INFO BANK

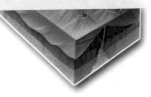

GEOGRAPHY

First published by Miles Kelly Publishing Ltd
Bardfield Centre, Great Bardfield
Essex, CM7 4SL

2 4 6 8 10 9 7 5 3 1

Editor
Isla MacCuish

Designer
Venita Kidwai

Editorial Director
Paula Borton

Art Director
Clare Sleven

Picture Research
Liberty Newton

British Library Cataloguing-in-Publication Data
A catalogue record for this book is available from the British Library

ISBN 1-84236-055-8
Printed in Hong Kong

www.mileskelly.net
info@mileskelly.net

Acknowledgements

The publishers would like to thank the following artists whose work appears in this book:

C M Buzer/Studio Galante, Kuo Kang Chen, Peter Dennis, Nick Farmer, Mike Foster, John James,
Malting Partnership, Janos Marffy, Martin Sanders, Francesco Spadori/Studio Galante, Mike White.

The publishers would like to thank the following sources for the photographs used in this book:

Page 20-21 (L) Stephanie Maze/Corbis; Page 22-23 (T/R) Ted Spiegel/Corbis; Page 26-27 (L) Paul Almasy/Corbis;
Page 28-29 (R) CRDPHOTO/Corbis; Page 34-35 (R) John Hestletine/Corbis; Page 58-59 (R) David Turnley/Corbis;
Page 58-59 (C) Keren Su/Corbis; Page 78-79 (T/R) Wolfgang Kaehler/Corbis; Page 82-83 (C) Galen Rowell/Corbis;
Page 84-85 (T/R)Reuters New Media Inc/Corbis; Page 88-89 (B/C) Graham Neden Ecoscene/Corbis;

All other photographs from Miles Kelly archives

INFO BANK

GEOGRAPHY

CLIVE CARPENTER

MiLes KeLLy
PUBLISHING

CONTENTS

CENTRAL & SOUTHERN AFRICA

NORTHERN ASIA

SOUTHERN ASIA

OCEANIA

POLAR REGIONS

AROUND THE WORLD

North America

Fewer than one person in ten in the world lives in North America, yet it is the powerhouse of the world. The USA has the biggest economy on Earth. America's mineral-rich northern neighbour, Canada, is one of the most prosperous countries in the world.

Central and South America

The mountains, jungles and plains of much of Central and South America have relatively few people. But the coasts and river valleys of the Spanish- and Portuguese-speaking countries of Latin America are also home to fast-expanding cities and a rapidly-growing population.

Northern Europe

A small region, Northern Europe has influence throughout the world. A good climate and plentiful natural resources encouraged human settlement and development. Modern industry began in Northern Europe and today standards of living are among the highest in the world.

Southern Europe

The coastline of the Mediterranean Sea is cut into by deep bays and dotted with islands. Along its shores, the towns of Southern Europe are ancient and attractive. Today, it is one of the world's most popular regions for tourists. But it was once the birthplace of great civilisations.

North Africa and the Middle East

Some of the world's oldest civilisations began in the river valleys of North Africa and the Middle East. Christianity and Islam also began in this region. In modern times, this region was relatively poor and undeveloped until the discovery of oil and natural gas in the 20th century.

Central and Southern Africa

In the last century, Central and Southern Africa have probably seen more changes than any other part of the Earth. This is a region of new countries, with cities and industries where once there was none. But this is also a region facing great problems – poverty, disease and wars.

Northern Asia

Northern Asia is a region of great contrasts and nearly one-quarter of the world's people. It contains China, the country with the largest population, and some of the world's greatest industrial nations, such as Japan and Korea.

Southern Asia

Southern Asia is home to over one-quarter of the world's population. Over one half of the people who live in Southern Asia are involved in farming. But the region also has huge cities and some of the most rapidly growing industries in the world.

Oceania

The Pacific Ocean occupies one-third of the Earth's surface. Across its waters are many islands – several large ones (Australia, New Guinea and the two main islands of New Zealand) and thousands of tiny islands. Together these lands form the continent of Oceania.

Polar regions

The polar regions are empty lands – too cold for many people to want to live there and too cold for farming. Yet under the ice and snow are natural riches – oil, natural gas, coal and metals – that may, one day, attract people to these regions.

HOW TO USE THE SUBJECT LINKS

Navigate your way through this book using the colour-coded bars located in the bottom right hand corner of every spread. Flip through the pages, matching colours and sub-headings, and you can compare and contrast themes such as environment, industry and famous places across ten different geographical areas.

Flip the pages and match the corner bars by colour. Make the links between ten different geographical topics.

NORTH AMERICA

A strong economy
The U.S. is self-sufficient in most products. It has the raw materials for nearly everything it needs. Principal industries include iron and steel, electrical and food.

Wall Street
The United States has the largest economy of any nation on Earth. Wall Street (right), in New York City, is its financial centre, housing the world's biggest stock exchange and many banks.

HOLLYWOOD

Shop, shop, shop!
Industry does not just mean making things. The biggest employer in the U.S. now is service industries – shops, hotels, catering, leisure, finance, etc. Service industries involve about three-quarters of the U.S. labour force and one of the largest sections is shopping. America gave the modern shopping mall to the world.

The silver screen
In the early days of film, the sunlight of California attracted movie-makers who filmed largely outdoors. Hollywood, Las Angeles, became the world's film capital and later attracted television. Yet now Bombay, India makes more films.

INDUSTRY

SOUTHERN ASIA

Family business
Most of India's cottage industries are worked by families.

Cottage industry
Home-based industry is called cottage industry. Nearly 300 million India's earn their living in home-based workshops, particularly in the carpet, textile, footwear and clothing industries. In India, these workshops are difficult to inspect and it is thought that at least 50 million children work in cottage industries.

Textile workers
Every fourth worker in India makes textiles. Textiles are used to make clothes, for export and for sale to tourists.

Petronas Towers
Standing at 492 metres, the 88-storey Petronas Towers dominate the skyline of the capital of Malaysia, Kuala Lumpur. The tallest office buildings in the world, the Towers have become a symbol of Malaysia's economic growth.

Cheap labour
Industry in much of South Asia is traditionally small scale and requiring lots of workers rather than machinery. This is the case in India and Pakistan where there is not the demand for so many modern goods – many people cannot afford them. Over one-third of India's population lives below the official poverty line. But other countries such as Thailand and Malaysia have been so successful that they are called 'tiger economies'. Big companies from Japan and Taiwan have invested in these countries, setting up factories to make parts for their industries more cheaply than they can do at home.

Spinning for profit
Silk is obtained from the webs spun by silkworms. Keeping silk worms has been a traditional activity in some cooler parts of Southern Asia, but the region is now important for the production of artificial silk in factories using cheap labour.

Dotcom
Some South Asian countries have adopted the Internet and modern computer technology eagerly. Singapore, for example, aims to put every citizen on the Internet. By 2005 at least 90% of the population will have been 'wired'.

INDUSTRY

Bingham Canyon copper mine
Canada and the US have some the world's biggest concentrations of valuable minerals – coal, oil, iron ore, bauxite, copper, silver and zinc. Some minerals, such as copper, are mined in pits like the massive copper mine at Bingham Canyon, near Salt Lake City (left).

A wealth of resources

The USA is self-sufficient in most minerals apart from oil and a few metals. The largest American oilfield is now in the Gulf of Mexico, off the coast of Texas, where there are drills and rigs at sea. But the most potential in the US is in the north of Alaska where very large deposits of oil and natural gas have been found. However, extracting oil in cold conditions would present extra problems.

Vital mineral
Oil is the most valuable mineral resource in Texas – the state produces about one quarter of the United States' oil.

Overfishing

The mixing of currents in the shallow seas off eastern Canada produces the ideal conditions for the tiny creatures that are the main food of vast shoals of fish. But too many fish have been taken and now there are not enough to reproduce and replace stocks. As a result many small Canadian fishing ports have had to stop fishing.

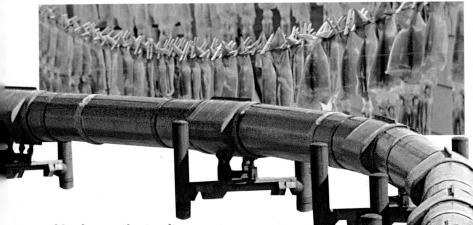

Preserving the catch
In the small ports of Newfoundland, Canada, fish used to be hung out to dry to preserve it. Now almost all of the (much-reduced) catch is frozen on the fishing ships.

Alaskan oil pipeline
Oil has to be brought long distances by pipeline to where it is needed. But to bring oil from northern Alaska has involved building through protected areas and national parks.

Pioneers of leisure

America 'invented' the modern leisure park such as Disneyworld, Disneyland and Epcot. More than half of all Americans visit an amusement park at least once a year. The USA also pioneered the idea of the national park – an area of natural beauty protected from development. Among the most visited is the Golden Gate National Park. Spectacular landscapes are also a draw for visitors, such as the Grand Canyon or Niagara Falls.

Famous bridge

The Golden Gate National Park is home to the bridge of the same name (right), which is one of the longest suspension bridges in the world.

International waterfall

Niagara Falls consists of two waterfalls – the American Falls in the United States and the Horseshoe Falls in Canada. The Niagara river forms a natural border between the two countries.

Appetite for height

The tallest structure in the world is the CN Tower in Toronto, Canada. 553 m tall, the 130,000-tonne concrete tower is topped by a revolving restaurant. On a clear day, it is possible to see hills 120 km away while dining.

Gateway to the west

The 'Wild West' is an attraction both for its scenery and history. The so-called 'gateway to the West' is the city of St Louis, which now has a real gateway – a steel-covered arch 192 m high.

Grand Canyon

The Grand Canyon in Arizona has been carved out by the Colorado River. It is 446 km long, 1.6 km deep, varies between 1 to 29 km wide. The Canyon is now part of a national park.

FAMOUS PLACES

Earthmoving

The outer layer of our planet (the crust) is divided into about 15 sections called 'tectonic plates'. These plates 'float' on top of a molten layer beneath. Plates move very slowly – a few millimetres a year on average. Where these plates collide, the Earth's surface is compressed and buckles up to form mountains, known as 'fold' mountains. The Alps were formed by the African plate moving northwards into the Eurasian Plate. And the Rocky Mountains formed where the Pacific Plate pressed against the North American Plate. The Rocky Mountains are still slowly rising as the pressure between the two plates continues. All the world's biggest mountain ranges are on the edges of plates.

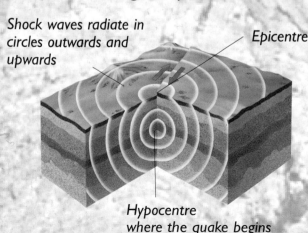

Shock waves radiate in circles outwards and upwards

Epicentre

Hypocentre where the quake begins

What makes the earth quake

The boundaries between plates (above) are often earthquake zones. In California, two plates are slowly sliding against one another along the San Andreas Fault. These plates lock together – for hundreds of years in places. The pressure builds up. Then suddenly, the plates slip past each other to create a major earthquake (left).

Pop-up mountains

Not all mountains are fold mountains, formed where plates press against one another. Some mountain ranges – far away from the edges of plates – are the result of plates moving elsewhere. Pressure makes mountains 'pop up' between huge cracks (faults). Examples in the USA include the Black Hills of Dakota and the Adirondack Mountains of New York State.

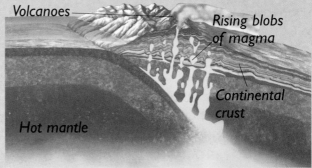

Volcanoes

Rising blobs of magma

Continental crust

Hot mantle

Jagged edge

The Rocky Mountains run down western North America for about 4800 km. They contain the highest peak in Canada (Mount Logan) and in the United States (Mount McKinley). They look jagged because water freezes in cracks and forces rocks to break apart.

Left standing

No matter how high a mountain, it will eventually be worn away by erosion. Rain washes away small grit. Rivers eat away valleys. Yet, in places, a layer of very hard rock will not be worn away so easily. This has happened in the American West where dramatic tall pillars, topped by hard rock, have been left standing, while softer material has been eroded away on either side.

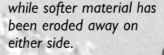

A strong economy

The U.S. is self-sufficient in most products. It has the raw materials for nearly everything it needs. Principal industries include iron and steel, motor vehicles, electrical and electronic engineering, food processing, chemicals, cement, aluminium, aerospace industries, telecommunications, textiles and clothing, and consumer goods. America's economy is half as big again as its nearest rival, Japan. The strength of that economy, and of its currency, the dollar, allows the U.S. to dominate the world.

Wall Street

The United States has the largest economy of any nation on Earth. Wall Street (right), in New York City, is its financial centre, housing the world's biggest stock exchange and many banks.

Dotcom

The Internet developed in America. Many computing companies are based on the West Coast, in Seattle or in 'Silicon Valley', California. It was thought much business in the 21st century would be Internet-based, but this has not happened.

Mass production

In 1908, American industrialist Henry Ford introduced mass-production, the assembly-line factory. Cars could be made quickly and cheaply. The motor vehicle industry is one of the largest in North America.

Shop, shop, shop!

Industry does not just mean making things. The biggest employer in the U.S. now is service industries – shops, hotels, catering, leisure, finance, etc. Service industries involve about three-quarters of the U.S. labour force and one of the largest sections is shopping. America gave the modern shopping mall to the world.

The silver screen

In the early days of film, the sunlight of California attracted movie-makers who filmed largely outdoors. Hollywood, Los Angeles, became the world's film capital and later attracted television. Yet now Bombay, India makes more films.

INDUSTRY

The life of a river

Rivers get their water from rainfall and melting snow. Most rivers are joined by other, smaller rivers along their course, called tributaries. The area draining into one river is called a drainage basin – the largest is the Amazon Basin in Brazil. A river carries a load of mud, stones and plant remains that it has eroded and picked up from the ground it flows over. When it slows down near the sea this material is often deposited in the form of land, called a delta. The Amazon Delta is the largest in the world.

Lake in the clouds
At just over 3800 m above sea level, the world's highest navigable lake is Lake Titicaca in Bolivia. Local people use reed boats (above) for transport around the lake.

Rain clouds

Water evaporates from sea

Delta

Tributary

Meander

Lifecycle of a river

Waterpower

Rivers are 'harnessed' to generate electricity. Dams are constructed to hold back artificial lakes (reservoirs). Water is dropped from the top of the dam to turn turbines to produce electricity. One of the world's largest dams is the Itaipu Dam on the Paraná River where Paraguay meets Brazil.

No rain terrain

In the north of Chile and southern Peru lies the Atacama Desert (below), the driest place on Earth. The Atacama is a desert because no moist air blows on to it from the adjoining ocean to fall as rain.

Iguazú Falls

Where rivers reach a fault or an area of soft rock, they often tumble over it to form a waterfall. The Iguazú Falls, forming a natural border between Brazil and Argentina, is one of the world's largest waterfalls in terms of the amount of water that flows over it. But downstream is a 'lost' waterfall – the larger Guaira Falls which were covered by a reservoir.

A better life

The rapidly growing cities in this region are busy, polluted and crowded with slum housing. São Paolo, Buenos Aires and Rio de Janeiro, all in South America, are among the world's largest cities. Millions of people in Central and Southern America want to move north to the USA to improve their lives. America tries to keep out many of these immigrants – there are just not enough jobs and houses in America for them all.

Border defence

Every year between 800,000 and 2,000,000 people from Central and Southern America enter the US illegally. Most of these people come from Mexico. The US/Mexican border has strict controls to try to prevent this.

Housing the poor

Bogota, the capital city of Colombia, and Rio de Janeiro (below) have many of the problems of the large cities of South America. These cities have grown so quickly that there is not enough housing. The city centres have stunning modern skyscrapers, but around the fringes there are poor shantytowns.

Mexico is a relatively short flight from the large cities of western USA. Resorts in Mexico offer a cheaper holiday for American tourists, as well as beautiful scenery and the attraction of being in another country. Acapulco was a small village 100 years ago, but is now a bustling seaside resort with more than half a million people.

Growing cities

The last 100 years has been a time when huge cities have grown. Farming has used more machinery and needed a smaller labour force while industry in towns has increased, requiring more workers. In 1900, only 12 cities in the world had more than 1,000,000 inhabitants. Now more than 300 cities house over 1,000,000 people. Some of the biggest of these cities are in Central and South America.

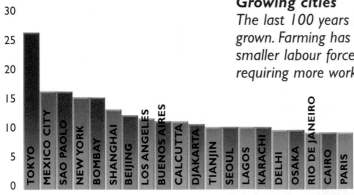

30
25
20
15
10
5
0
Millions

TOKYO, MEXICO CITY, SAO PAOLO, NEW YORK, BOMBAY, SHANGHAI, BEIJING, LOS ANGELES, BUENOS AIRES, CALCUTTA, DJAKARTA, TIANJIN, SEOUL, LAGOS, KARACHI, DELHI, OSAKA, RIO DE JANEIRO, CAIRO, PARIS

Population explosion

Central and South America have seen an enormous population growth in the last 100 years – from just over 50 million in 1900 to more than 500 million by the year 2000. Cities have grown, industries have flourished and nearly half of the forests that once covered the region have been cut down. The result has been pollution on a huge scale, with poisoned rivers and slums surrounding the cities.

Unexplored regions

South America contains some of the world's last unexplored places. The Amazon Basin is still being explored for minerals. For this, roads and airstrips are built. This invasion destroys forests and threatens the way of life of tribes who live there, like the Yanomami. They live uncomplicated lives, taking from the forest only what they need for food and shelter.

Yanomami family at home

Urban waste

The world is running out of places to put rubbish such as packaging. Recycling breaks down rubbish into raw materials to use again. In Mexico City, what the rich throw away as rubbish the poor often retrieve from dumps to reuse.

Choking cities

Streets of the cities of Central and South America are filled with vehicles. Fumes from car exhaust gases pollute the air and are the main part of the smog that blankets some cities. Mexico City is particularly badly affected because its centre lies in a basin in which the smog becomes trapped.

Deforestation

The Amazon Basin contains the world's largest tropical rainforest. But every year an area about half the size of Scotland is cleared and then burned to make new farmland for Brazil's many landless peasants. Many plant and animal species lose their habitat and become extinct.

ENVIRONMENT

Land of contrasts

Central and Southern America is a region of tropical jungles, sub-tropical forest, deserts, and mountains. But in the south – in Argentina, Uruguay and southern Brazil – lies one of the world's great farming regions. Grasslands provide pasture for beef in the pampas and for sheep in the cooler Patagonia. In the eastern hills and coastal regions of Brazil are farms that specialise in a single crop – usually either coffee or cocoa.

New discoveries

When Europeans rediscovered the Americas in the 1400s they found not only new lands – they discovered a range of new crops that were to change the lives of Europeans. Can you imagine what it was like without cocoa (from Mexico), maize (Mexico) and potatoes (Peru). The explorer Christopher Columbus discovered tobacco (right) in Cuba in 1492. Since then its cultivation has spread around the world.

Home on the Range

The flat open plains of Argentina and Uruguay are called pampas. These plains are ranching country: gauchos are modern-day South American cowboys. Ranches (called estancias) employ many people to tend cattle, but wheat and maize farming now employ far fewer owing to the huge combines and other machinery used.

Maize farming

The pampas are important for maize (corn). Maize is a native of Central America. It grows to 4.5 m high and is used for animal feed, oil, breakfast cereal and as a vegetable. After wheat and rice, it is the third most important cereal crop in the world.

World's maize producers

China (8%)

France (12%)

Argentina (15%)

USA (65%)

FARMING & FORESTRY

Commuter culture

One quarter of the world's industries are concentrated in Northern Europe which is a densely populated region. The southern part of the Netherlands (where many people are crammed in a small area), the Ruhr industrial area in Germany, and London and Paris are overcrowded. People are living farther from their work. But good roads (for example German autobahns) and railway systems allow people to live in smaller towns and to travel into the big cities to work – commuting.

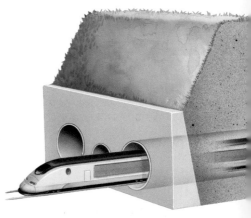

Leisure time

A high standard of living – and a low age at which people retire from work – means that people in northern Europe have plenty of leisure time. In Belgium, Finland and France, for example, most people retire below age 60.

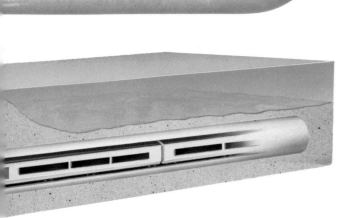

Channel Tunnel
It takes 20 minutes to travel from Britain to France by the Eurostar train through the Channel Tunnel. The tunnel is nearly 50 km long, 37 km underwater.

Percentages of Europeans living in the countryside

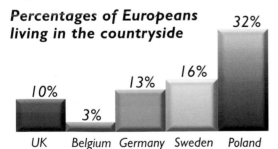

UK	Belgium	Germany	Sweden	Poland
10%	3%	13%	16%	32%

In Poland about a quarter of the nation's workforce is employed in agriculture. Many of the farms are small and worked on by the owners. The most important crops are sugar beet, potatoes and cereals.

Supermarkets
It is now unusual in Northern Europe to find many food shops in city centres. Because most people have cars, giant supermarkets have been built in the outskirts of large towns.

Average National Incomes
Luxembourg £33,100 (the highest in the world), Switzerland £27,800, Norway £27,600, Denmark £25,100, Sweden £21,900, Finland £21,500 and Germany £21,100.

Natural Power Sources

The natural heat of the Earth can be used to produce power. In Iceland, where geysers shoot steam into the sky, water from hot springs is piped to heat all the buildings of the capital, Reykjavik. This hot water also warms greenhouses, which make Iceland almost self-sufficient in vegetables for salads. But there are very few places in the world like Iceland where natural heat from our planet can be used in this way.

Eruption of steam
Geysers occur when cold underground water reaches rocks that are hot. The water heats to form steam, which then erupts from the earth in a tall column.

Water Power

Water power in Europe once meant water wheels built across small streams to power mills. In the 18th century the huge coal deposits of the continent began to be used and industries moved to coalfields. Now, water power is important again. In northern Europe many deep narrow valleys have been dammed. This dam is in Scotland, but Norway and Sweden are greater producers of electricity from dams.

Fossilization

Coal is a fossil. It is made from the remains of plants that lived millions of years ago. Fossils form where plant or animal remains laid down in rocks are gradually replaced with dissolved minerals over millions of years. In coal, the plant material has been crushed to form a hard deposit.

Natural Gas

Gas, like coal and oil, is also what is referred to as a 'fossil fuel'. It was also formed over a period of millions of years, from the bodies of millions of plankton in the sea, slowly changing into oil and gas by being compressed and heated under the weight of rocks.

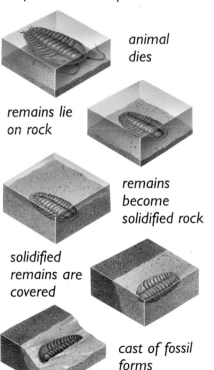

animal dies

remains lie on rock

remains become solidified rock

solidified remains are covered

cast of fossil forms

NATURAL RICHES

NORTHERN EUROPE

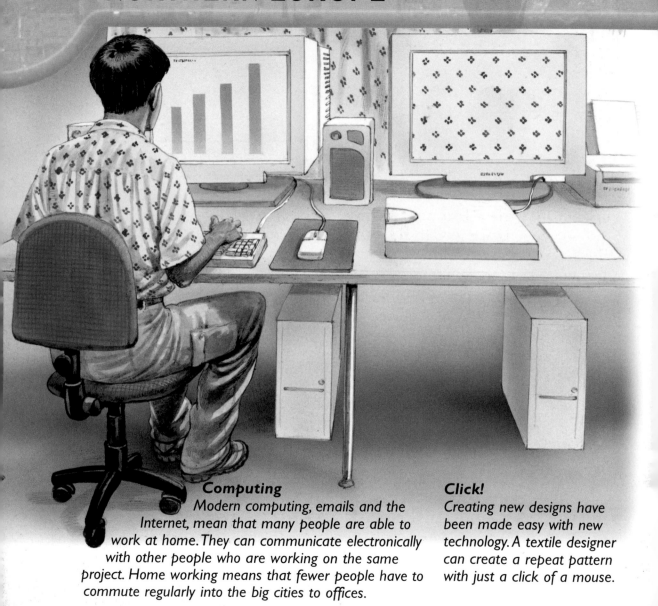

Computing
Modern computing, emails and the Internet, mean that many people are able to work at home. They can communicate electronically with other people who are working on the same project. Home working means that fewer people have to commute regularly into the big cities to offices.

Click!
Creating new designs have been made easy with new technology. A textile designer can create a repeat pattern with just a click of a mouse.

Under threat

Northern Europe was the world's first great industrial region. But it didn't have all the raw materials it needed. European industry relied on trade (and in the past on trade with colonies). Today, Europe's industries are under threat from places where workers are cheaper. For example, much of Northern Europe's textile industry has disappeared unable to compete with Asia.

Coal mining
Modern industry began in Northern Europe at the end of the 18th century. Coal was used to power factories and Europe's great industrial areas grew up on coalfields.

City of London
The City of London is the financial centre of Europe, with the continent's largest stock exchange and the headquarters of many banks. The reasons are historic. In the 19th century, Britain was the major economic and industrial power in Europe.

The largest port
The Dutch port of Rotterdam is the largest port in the world. It grew as the principal port for Europe's greatest industrial region, the Ruhr in north-west Germany.

INDUSTRY

European upheaval

Northern Europe has seen major changes in the past century. Two World Wars were fought in Northern Europe from 1914 until 1918 and then 1939 until 1945. After the Second World War, Russia (then known as the Soviet Union) set up Communist governments in Eastern Europe. But the Communist system did not work, and the countries ruled by the Communists fell further and further behind Western Europe. Between 1989 and 1991, these Communist governments collapsed. Europe started to become one again.

Changes in Europe

During the 1900s, after two world wars, Europe underwent huge political changes. A Communist government took control in Russia, 1917. This new Soviet Union came to dominate eastern countries. But in 1991 when the Soviet Union collapsed, more than 10 countries gained the freedom to become independent.

Europe, 1914

Europe, 2000

From east to west

Since the 'Iron Curtain' (a divide between the countries in eastern Europe and those in western Europe) came down, the people of eastern Europe have been freer to move within the continent. Many thousands of people from the east – and particularly from the poorer countries in south-eastern Europe like Albania and Romania – have moved to the richer countries of north-western Europe in search of better jobs, better homes and better lives. These people are known as 'economic refugees'. Their arrival in a new country – sometimes illegally – has caused some problems and resentment even though there are jobs for them in Northern Europe.

Changing Boundaries

Germany, divided in two since 1945, was reunited in 1990. The Soviet Union broke up into 15 countries as Russia's grip on the peoples it ruled loosened. Estonia, Latvia and Lithuania, among others, broke away from Russia to become independent European countries. Yugoslavia was split up in a series of wars.

The Berlin wall

For nearly 50 years Germany was split by a wall that stopped people fleeing to the west from the communist east. The wall physically divided the city of Berlin. When Communism eventually collapsed, the wall was torn down in 1990. Only small, ruined sections still remain.

European Union

In the 1950s, the countries of western Europe formed a trading organization, now called the European Union. Since then this group has become closer and includes Austria, Belgium (whose capital Brussels, left, is the EU's headquarters), Denmark, Finland, France, Germany, Greece, Ireland, Italy, Luxembourg, the Netherlands, Portugal, Spain, Sweden and the UK.

Tourist attractions

Eastern Mediterranean countries such as Greece and Turkey are much hotter in summer than the west, which is nearer the cooling influence of the wide Atlantic Ocean. These high temperatures and dry weather attract many tourists from northern Europe to the Mediterranean beaches.

Autumn storms

Mediterranean winters can be wet, but often the greatest amount of rain in southern Europe comes in thunderstorms in the autumn, when spectacular lightning displays light the sky.

Angle of sunlight

The big seasonal difference in temperature is due to the movement of the overhead

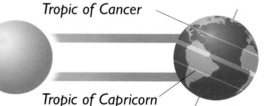

Tropic of Cancer

Tropic of Capricorn

Sun. When the Mediterranean is nearest to the Sun in midsummer it is hottest and driest. The coolest time of year comes when the Sun is farthest away from the Mediterranean, and closer to the southern hemisphere.

Microclimates

Because of the many bays lining the Mediterranean coast, and the mountains surrounding it, there are lots of local variations in the weather, which would otherwise be quite predictable.

Climate types

- Mountains
- Temperate forest
- Desert

Hot air and cold winds

Southern Europe – the area north of the Mediterranean Sea – has what is called a 'Mediterranean' climate. This type of climate has mild, wet winters and hot, dry summers. Some parts of the Mediterranean get extremely hot in summer. This heats up the air which then rises. To take its place, cooler air rushes in from nearby. This causes the many strong local winds for which the Mediterranean is famous. One example is the Mistral, a cold dry wind that blows down the Rhône valley in France towards the Mediterranean. This lowers the temperature in late autumn and early winter.

Sun-soaked slopes

Winter rain is stored in reservoirs and tanks and is used in spring and summer to irrigate the fruit for which Southern Europe is famous. On sunny south-facing slopes farmers have for centuries grown vines, olives, oranges and lemons.

Weather in Athens, Greece

Average temperature:
11°C – December
26°C – June

Average rainfall:
137 mm – December
18 mm – June

Walled towns

The old towns of the Mediterranean shores and inland were built on hills to avoid low-lying marshes where mosquitoes bred. In the Middle Ages, to avoid attacks by pirates and others these towns were walled so that they could be easily defended. As a result these traditional towns were quite cramped with little room to spare for gardens. Streets are narrow and often steep because it is hilly.

Holy days

Living so close together people tend to be sociable. Many towns have festivals, often when different parts of the town compete against each other. Festivals include bull running in Spain and horse races through streets in Italy.

Siesta

The working day begins early before it gets too hot and shops often close for several hours at midday. Many have an afternoon snooze – siesta – and then enjoy eating outdoors later.

Special Days

Most of Southern Europe is Catholic. The Catholic Church has many special days, including saints' days when there are processions and other festivities where statues of saints are carried through streets. Although many do not actually go to church now, traditional religious festivals still play an important part in people's lives.

SOUTHERN EUROPE

A juicy industry

Orange groves are part of the Mediterranean scene. Each tree produces about 70 kilos of oranges a year. Spain, Italy and Greece are among the world's top ten producers.

Olives

The olive is grown for its tiny 'berry' crushed to make oil for cooking as well as to eat as a 'fruit'. The small trees are tolerant of different soils but don't like standing in wet soil, so the Mediterranean slopes are ideal.

Health & Diet

Olive oil is an important part of Mediterranean cooking which features fresh fruit and vegetables and plenty of fish. This healthy diet helps Southern Europeans live a long healthy life.

Small farms

Southern Europe has a Mediterranean climate – hot dry summer, cooler winter with some rain. It is a region of many small farms, some only a couple of hectares or fewer. Soils can be poor and rocky and the land is often steep. But south-facing slopes can be used for olive groves and vineyards and flatter areas, with better soil, are used for orange groves, lemon groves and a wide variety of vegetables. Some slopes are terraced.

World's olive producers

Other (28%)

Italy (26%)

Spain (33%)

Greece (13%)

Irrigation

Because rainfall is low – and in summer often almost non-existent – irrigation is important. Water from the autumn thunderstorms and winter rains is stored in tanks and reservoirs and piped to the fields in late spring and summer.

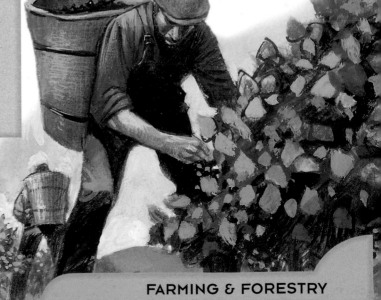

FARMING & FORESTRY

Ruins in cities

Southern Europe was the birthplace of two great civilizations, the ancient Greeks and the Romans. Temples, aqueducts, walls, palaces and other ancient remains are found throughout the region. Nowhere are they more spectacular than Rome, in Italy, or Athens, in Greece. In central Rome is the forum, the marketplace of ancient Rome, surrounded by temples. Athens is overlooked by a hill town (the acropolis) and its famous temple, the Parthenon.

Tourist attractions

Southern Europe is one of the major tourist regions of the world. People were first attracted in great numbers from northern Europe in the 1960s by cheap holidays in a region where dry sunny summer weather is almost guaranteed. Spain, where the tourism industry employs 1.5 million people, is the main destination, receiving 70 million visitors every year.

Ruined temple

The Parthenon was constructed from white marble to honour Athena, the goddess of Athens. All the sculptures that once covered it have been taken away or destroyed.

Style capital

Spain's second city, Barcelona, is one of the most stylish places in Europe. Among its famous buildings is the unfinished church of the Sagrada Familia (below). The city adjoins the bustling holiday resorts of the Costa Brava.

Smallest country

The Vatican City, home of the Pope and headquarters of the Roman Catholic Church, is the smallest country in the world. Dominated by the dome of St Peter's Cathedral, the tiny Vatican City draws millions of Catholic pilgrims every year.

Istanbul

Istanbul is one of the main sights of Turkey, a country that attracts 10 million visitors a year. Some are drawn to the beaches, others to the low price of holidays – things are much cheaper than in Northern Europe. A string of ruined ancient Greek and Roman cities attracts visitors, as well as mosques like the Hagia Sofia (right).

Royal monuments

The ancient civilizations of the Near East left remarkable monuments behind. Among the most famous are the Great Pyramids in Egypt, which are around 4500 years old. Built by the pharaohs (kings) of Egypt as tombs, the pyramids are also thought to record the pattern of the stars in the sky. Next to the pyramids is the even older Sphinx, a stone lion with a human face. These ancient remains attract nearly 4 million tourists every year.

Legendary animal
The Giant Sphinx – 20 m high – is the largest of thousands of sphinxes, many of which have wings and the head of a hawk.

The vast empire of Persepolis was capital of the Persian empire, stretching from Greece to India 2500 years ago.

Off the map

Some of the historic sites in this region are not yet famous in the wider world. For various reasons, both religious and political, these places are off the tourist map. Iraq is isolated for political reasons, so no tourists visit the remains of ancient Babylon. Since the Islamic Revolution in Iran, few outsiders have visited the stunning ruins of Persepolis there.

Great Mosque, Mali

Many of the ancient buildings in Northern Africa were built as places of worship. The Great Mosque at Djenne, in Mali, is the largest mud-brick building in the world. Mud bricks do not last, so it has been rebuilt several times, most recently in 1905.

Istanbul

Built on either side of a narrow sea, Istanbul in Turkey is half in Europe, half in Asia. Founded by the Romans, Istanbul is famous for its palaces and mosques, as well as indoor markets, bazaars and grand architecture.

FAMOUS PLACES

From oasis to big city

Much of North Africa and the Middle East is desert. Farming is limited to river valleys, such as the densely populated Nile Valley in Egypt where river water is used for irrigation. People also live in some hilly areas with better rainfall and oases – isolated fertile patches in the desert where water is found. Otherwise big cities are on the coast where trade and industries are most developed. Oil and natural gas have transformed countries such as Saudi Arabia, Libya and the UAE. These countries do not have enough people to fill all the new jobs. So, people come from overpopulated poorer neighbours, such as Yemen and Palestine, to work.

Ship of the Desert
Camels are called 'ships of the desert' because they are suited to life in the dry sands of Arabia, where they can travel 50 km a day. Camels can go for days without water and their wide feet do not sink in the sand.

Dubai

Sixty years ago Dubai, in the UAE, was little more than a fishing village. Now it is a booming modern city with great highways, an airport, a massive container port, factories, gleaming fashionable shops and luxury hotels. All this has happened because the state of Dubai is rich in oil.

Shopping

The shopping areas of the cities of North Africa and the Middle East used to be bazaars – narrow streets lined with tiny shops and stalls. In the large cities the bazaars now mainly sell souvenirs to visitors.

HOW PEOPLE LIVE

Striking oil

Oil has brought development and riches into desert regions where previously, there was little reason for anyone to choose to live there. The Gulf coast of Saudi Arabia and the United Arab Emirates (UAE) is now lined with oilfields, modern ports and cities. To help run the fields, and to provide all kinds of services in the fast-developing and wealthy cities like Dubai, people have migrated from other parts of Asia and Europe: in the UAE over half the population comes from India and Pakistan.

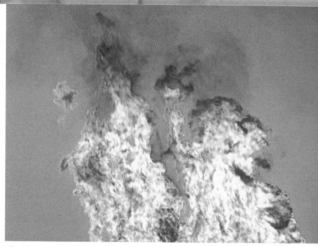

Oil wars
Oil caused wars in the 20th century. In 1990 Iraq invaded its small oil-rich neighbour Kuwait. A US-led force freed Kuwait in 1991 but retreating Iraqis set fire to Kuwait's oil wells.

Riches of the Desert
The huge expanse of the Saudi desert is dotted with oil refineries.

Oil distribution

Oil is the basis of modern industry and transport. But it is seldom found where it is needed. The major centres of the world's industry are in North America, western Europe and Japan – but the biggest oil-producing countries are in the Middle East.

Oil consumption

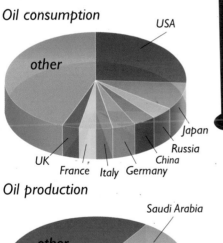

USA

other

Japan

Russia

China

Germany

Italy

France

UK

Oil production

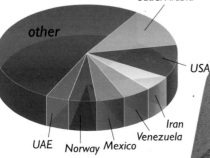

Saudi Arabia

other

USA

Iran

Venezuela

Mexico

Norway

UAE

Wealth and poverty

The oil states of the Gulf (Saudi Arabia, the UAE and Kuwait) and Libya have grown rich on oil. But the Middle East and North Africa is a region of contrasts. Whereas the Gulf states have a high standard of living, poverty remains in countries with little or no oil, such as Yemen.

Daily prayers

The main influence on people's lives in this region is religion – Islam. 'Islam' means submission – Muslims are people who submit themselves to Allah (God) by accepting Islam. Muslims pray five times a day. The call to prayer is broadcast from the minaret (tower) of a mosque. Attendance at a mosque is optional. But men usually go to the mosque on Friday.

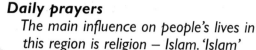

Diet and dress

Customs and diet are influenced by climate and religion. Flat bread, fruit and vegetables are important parts of the diet, but people do not eat pork for religious reasons. Long, loose clothing is designed to keep cool, but Islam also says women must wear modest clothes.

Holy cities

All Muslims who can afford to are expected to make the pilgrimage to the holy cities in Saudi Arabia, at least once. Each year millions of Muslims go on the pilgrimage (the hajj). They visit Mecca, the site of an ancient sacred rock (the Kaaba) and the city where the holy book of Islam, the Qu'ran, was revealed to the Prophet Muhammad. The hajj also involves visiting Medina, the city to which Muhammad fled in 622.

Wailing Wall

The Wailing Wall in Jerusalem is practically all that remains of the Temple of Solomon, built in Biblical times. Jews pray at the Wall.

Conflict

There is continuing violence in the Holy Land between Israel and the Palestinians. The area is home to both, but they cannot yet agree a compromise to divide the land between them and to live peacefully as neighbours.

Dome of the Rock

The mosque on the Dome of the Rock dominates Jerusalem, a holy city to three world religions: Christianity, Islam and Judaism. Its future is contested by Israel, which says that Jerusalem is its capital, and by the Palestinians, who want it to be theirs.

Plantations

Many of the crops exported from Central and Southern Africa come from plantations – very large farms, most originally owned by foreigners in the period when African countries were colonies of European countries. Foreign companies still own many plantations but more land is returning to African ownership. The Ivory Coast in West Africa is the largest producer of cacao in the world.

World's cacao producers

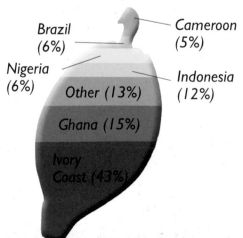

Brazil (6%)

Cameroon (5%)

Nigeria (6%)

Other (13%)

Indonesia (12%)

Ghana (15%)

Ivory Coast (43%)

Cash for crops
More African farmers grow crops to sell – cash crops – as well as food for themselves. These crops include coffee, cacao (which produces cocoa) and bananas.

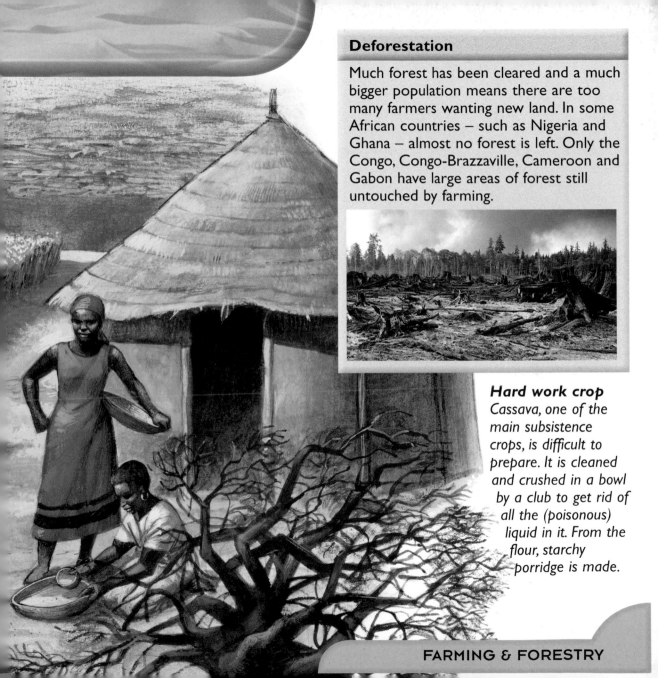

Deforestation

Much forest has been cleared and a much bigger population means there are too many farmers wanting new land. In some African countries – such as Nigeria and Ghana – almost no forest is left. Only the Congo, Congo-Brazzaville, Cameroon and Gabon have large areas of forest still untouched by farming.

Hard work crop

Cassava, one of the main subsistence crops, is difficult to prepare. It is cleaned and crushed in a bowl by a club to get rid of all the (poisonous) liquid in it. From the flour, starchy porridge is made.

FARMING & FORESTRY

A stable climate

Because most of this region is near the Equator much of Africa is hot all year. And because inland Africa is mainly flat plains, rather than high ranges of mountains that would form barriers against the movement of air, the climate is very similar over wide areas. In countries nearest to the Equator, the climate is much the same all year round – hot and wet. Mornings are clear, but by midday clouds have started to form, and by late afternoon, or early evening, thunderstorms begin and there is heavy rain.

Weather in the savannah

 Bulawayo, Zimbabwe
Average temperature:
23°C – December
15°C – June

Average rainfall:
124 mm – December
2 mm – June

Open grassland

In the areas around the rainforest are the tropical grasslands called savannah. Trees and bushes are scarce and new grass grows only when the rainy season comes.

Weather in the rainforest

 Gemena, Congo
Average temperature:
26°C – December
26°C – June

Average rainfall:
168 mm – December
155 mm – June

Steamy rainforests

High temperatures and heavy rainfall are ideal for the growth of trees in a broad band of rainforest running across central Africa. Trees in the forest grow up to 45 m tall. Their topmost branches form a canopy that almost blots out the sunlight.

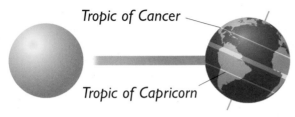

Tropic of Cancer

Tropic of Capricorn

Seasons

There is little seasonal variation in temperature near the Equator. Moving away from the Equator, there are seasons. The Sun is directly above the Equator during March and September, and above the Tropics of Cancer and Capricorn in June and December.

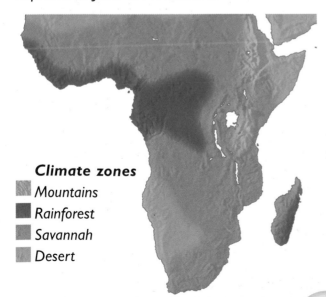

Climate zones
- Mountains
- Rainforest
- Savannah
- Desert

Lost forest

The forest is decreasing in size rapidly as it is felled for farming, destroying wildlife habitats and endangering plant species.

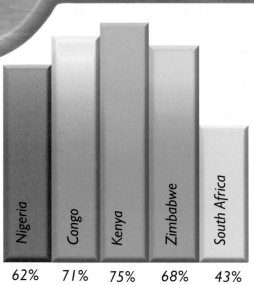

Nigeria	Congo	Kenya	Zimbabwe	South Africa
62%	71%	75%	68%	43%

Country dwellers

Most Africans are still farmers, herders and hunters. The percentage of people living in the country in typical African states is shown above

Town and country

Town life and country life in modern Africa are very different. In most African countries the majority of people live in the country. Only South Africa, which has more big cities and industries than any other African country, is an exception.

Women pounding cassava ready to cook

Harare

Towns in Africa have grown rapidly over the last 50 years. They attracted people from the countryside, but there are not enough jobs to go round. In Harare, Zimbabwe, over half the people do not have jobs.

Children playing in shade of baobab tree

Dried up river bed

Natural disasters

The countries of Central and Southern Africa are poor. Most of the 20 poorest nations are in Africa. Natural disasters add to the problems. Mozambique had terrible floods in 1999-2000. Severe droughts in Ethiopia and Somalia in the last 20 years meant that crops failed and many starved. And some countries – such as Rwanda and Sierra Leone – have suffered civil wars which have made many people refugees

Plains and deserts

Less than one third of Africa is forested – the rest is covered by either desert or tropical grassland called savannah. The Sahara, in the north, is the largest desert in the world. Partly because the climate is changing, and partly because people have damaged the land by trying to farm in dry areas next to the desert, the Sahara is spreading south into Central Africa. Savannah regions are great plains of tall grasses with isolated clumps of trees. These grasslands vary from very dry to wet and lush with the seasons.

Savannah wildlife
The savannah grasslands of Africa are home to giraffes and vast herds of zebras, gazelles, antelopes and wildebeest, as well as the lions and other big cats that feed upon them.

Ice at the Equator
Rising from the tropical grasslands of East Africa is Mount Kilimanjaro, the tallest mountain in Africa. Although it is near the Equator, its summit is high and cold enough to have an ice cap.

Moist air blows in from the sea

Water tank

The plants of the savannah are well adapted to life with one dry season and one wet season. The grasses die back in the dry season and spring up again when the rains come. Trees like the baobab (right) store water in their thick trunks to use during the drought.

'Rain shadow' effect desert formation

Deserts form when land does not receive moist winds from the sea. For example, in the Namib Desert in Southern Africa, a dry wind blows from the land out to the sea. Other deserts might lie beyond (in the shadow of) mountains, where the clouds rise over the peaks and deposit rainfall on one side of the mountain range, and are 'empty' when they reach the far side (below).

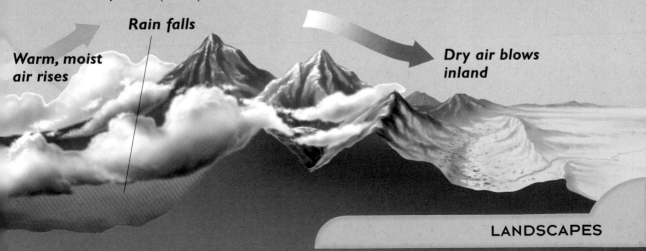

Rain falls

Warm, moist air rises

Dry air blows inland

Shrinking sea

The Aral Sea, in Kazakhstan and Uzbekistan, was once the world's fourth largest lake. But now it is less than half the size it was 40 years ago. The reason for this is that water from the two main rivers feeding the lake has been diverted to irrigate the cotton fields of Uzbekistan, and for use in cities. Not enough water reaches the lake to maintain it. So, year by year, the lake grows smaller – 135 of the 173 species of animals and fish that used to live in the lake have now become extinct and the surrounding land is becoming desert.

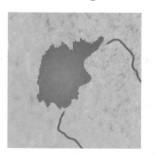 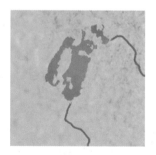

Aral Sea before and after
Compare the size and shape of the Aral Sea in the 1960s (left), when more river water flowed into it, and how it looks today (right) – split in two and still shrinking.

Changing boundaries

The countries of central northern Asia used to be ruled by Russia as part of the Soviet Union. But in 1991 the Soviet Union broke up into 15 independent countries. One of these new countries, Kazakhstan, the tenth largest country in the world in area – faces major problems of pollution from old factories.

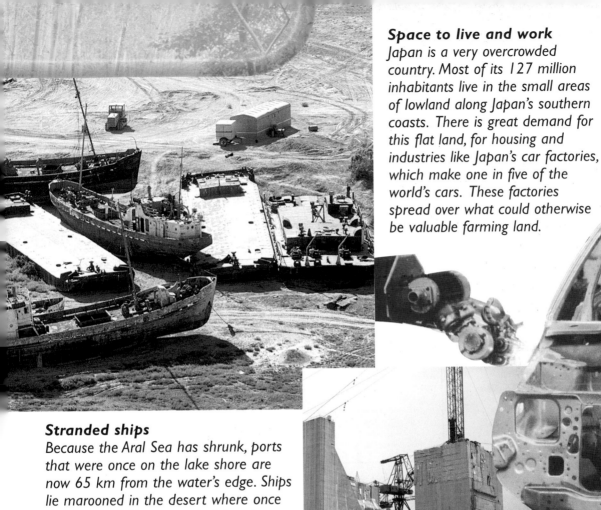

Space to live and work

Japan is a very overcrowded country. Most of its 127 million inhabitants live in the small areas of lowland along Japan's southern coasts. There is great demand for this flat land, for housing and industries like Japan's car factories, which make one in five of the world's cars. These factories spread over what could otherwise be valuable farming land.

Stranded ships

Because the Aral Sea has shrunk, ports that were once on the lake shore are now 65 km from the water's edge. Ships lie marooned in the desert where once there were fishing grounds (above).

Massive power station

The huge Three Gorges dam in China (right) is being built across China's longest river, the Chang Jiang. A giant reservoir of water 100 km across will provide the power to generate electricity.

ENVIRONMENT

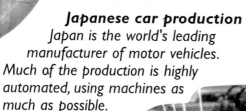

Japanese car production
Japan is the world's leading manufacturer of motor vehicles. Much of the production is highly automated, using machines as much as possible.

The big players
Northern Asia is home to the new industrial giants – China, Japan and South Korea. China's industry has relied on cheap workers to make cheap goods to export. But also relies on mineral and fuel resources. Japan has the second largest industrial economy in the world, but it has few natural resources. Japan relies on exports to survive and the country owes much of its success to research and new ideas.

Growing finance

The growth of industry has led to the development of major banks and stock exchanges in the region. The stock exchanges at Tokyo and Hong Kong are among the five largest in the world. And China, which did not have any stock exchanges a generation ago, now has four, including one at Shenzhen, a boom city near Hong Kong. Shenzhen has grown from a fishing village to a city of over 1 000,000 in 25 years.

Shanghai trade centre

China's largest city, Shanghai, is also the headquarters of many of the country's largest companies and the home of the main Chinese stock exchange. All along China's eastern and southern coasts industry is flourishing and cities expanding. In Shanghai's case, the city is growing rapidly — both outwards and upwards. Two of the world's highest office buildings are under construction in Shanghai and a whole new business district is being built.

Quality goods

The electrical goods industries of Northern Asia began by making cheap goods, for example in the island of Taiwan. But in the 1980s and 1990s the countries of this region started to specialise more in quality items . Japan, China and South Korea now lead the world in the production of electronic equipment and electrical goods.

INDUSTRY

Ancient sites

Northern Asia is a region full of amazing ancient ruins and monuments, like the famous 'army' of terracotta soldiers at Xian, in China. There is also breathtaking scenery such as the unique, pointy limestone peaks of southern China, or the icy wastes of Siberia in Russia. There may be much to see but taking holidays is a recent development in Northern Asia. In Japan, South Korea and parts of China, people are now becoming wealthy and have money to spend on travel. However, people take little leisure time and fewer holidays than is common in the West.

Tourists welcome

China is opening up to tourism. Twenty years ago, the Chinese government discouraged visitors. But now, nearly 10 million foreign tourists come to China every year. One of the main attractions in Beijing, the capital, is the Forbidden City, a vast complex of temples and palaces that was for centuries the home of Chinese emperors.

Great Wall of China

The Great Wall of China stretches for 3460 km across the dusty plains in the north of the country. The wall was built 2200 years ago, to keep out Mongol invaders from Central Asia. The wall varies between 5-16 m high and has a defensive tower positioned about every 60 m.

Modern attractions

Not all the famous buildings and sights of Northern Asia are ancient. China is now building some of the tallest skyscrapers in the world. Few cities have as many spectacular modern buildings as Hong Kong (right), which was once a British colony. Hong Kong is a major port, business and manufacturing centre.

Japanese sights

Japan attracts relatively few foreign tourists – it is a long way from North America and Western Europe, where most of the world's tourists come from. The snow-capped volcano Mount Fuji and the ancient remains at Kyoto (left) are popular places for Japanese tourists to visit.

Japanese village
Although 78% of Japanese people live in towns and cities, the warmer climate of the islands of Kyushi and Shikoki allows farming communities to thrive.

Rich and poor
This region contains some of the most exciting rapidly growing modern cities in the world – Shanghai, Tokyo, Seoul and Hong Kong. It also includes areas that are remote and poor, even within the same countries. Far western and north-western China is poor, while the cities of the south and east coasts of China have a high standard of living. And deep in Central Asia, countries like Uzbekistan and Tajikistan are very poor.

Hong Kong
Hong Kong has a standard of living almost as high as that of Northern European countries. Many people think the 21st century will be the 'Pacific Century', with the greatest increases in prosperity being along the Asian edge of the Pacific Ocean – in places like Hong Kong.

Scientists have proved a link between what we eat and our health. In Northern Asia, people eat more fish and vegetables. This healthy, low fat diet has helped the Japanese to become the longest-lived nation on Earth.

Traffic jams

Cities in Asia have grown so quickly that the transport has not had time to catch up. Most North Asian cities suffer from traffic gridlock – and where not everyone can afford a car, bicycle jams are common.

HOW PEOPLE LIVE

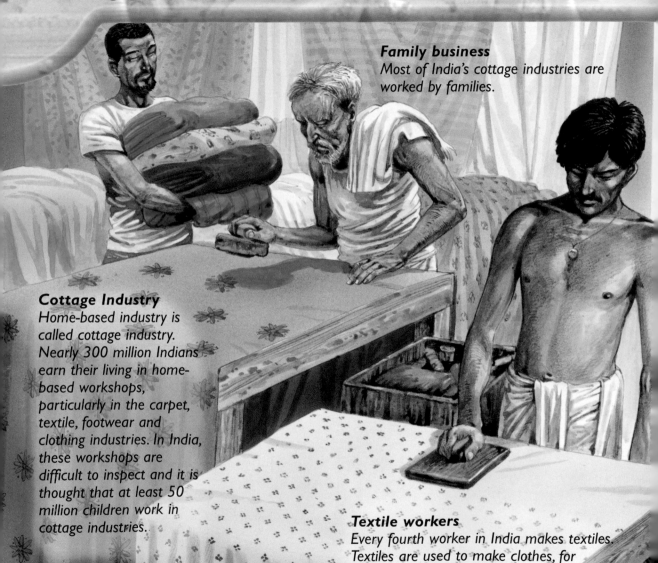

Family business
Most of India's cottage industries are worked by families.

Cottage Industry
Home-based industry is called cottage industry. Nearly 300 million Indians earn their living in home-based workshops, particularly in the carpet, textile, footwear and clothing industries. In India, these workshops are difficult to inspect and it is thought that at least 50 million children work in cottage industries.

Textile workers
Every fourth worker in India makes textiles. Textiles are used to make clothes, for export and for sale to tourists.

Petronas Towers

Standing at 492 metres, the 88-storey Petronas Towers dominate the skyline of the capital of Malaysia, Kuala Lumpur. The tallest office buildings in the world, the Towers have become a symbol of Malaysia's economic growth.

Spinning for profit

Silk is obtained from the webs spun by silkworms. Keeping silk worms has been a traditional activity in some cooler parts of Southern Asia. But the region is now important for the production of artificial silk in factories using cheap labour.

Cheap labour

Industry in much of South Asia is traditionally small scale and requiring lots of workers rather than machinery. This is the case in India and Pakistan where there is not the demand for so many modern goods – many people cannot afford them. Over one-third of India's population lives below the official poverty line. But other countries such as Thailand and Malaysia have been so successful that they are called 'tiger economies'. Big companies from Japan and Taiwan have invested in these countries, setting up factories to make parts for their industries more cheaply than they can do at home.

Dotcom

Some South Asian countries have adopted the Internet and modern computer technology eagerly. Singapore, for example, aims to put every citizen on the Internet. By 2005 at least 90% of the population will have been 'wired'.

Silk worm farms

Most of the world's silk is produced in Asia. Silk worms spin a cocoon, each of which contains more than 700 metres of thread. But it takes six kilograms of cocoons to make one kilogram of silk.

Tea picking

Tea is grown in the cooler hills of India and Sri Lanka. Many people work on tea plantations, picking the leaves from the tea bushes. Very many of the workers are women.

A rice diet

Southern Asia is one of the most densely populated regions on Earth. Many of the people rely upon one crop – rice. In fact, more than half of the world's population depends upon rice for food. Of the seven main producers of rice in the world, six are in Southern Asia. Scientists have worked to produce better varieties of rice that yield more grain. Since the 1960s the yield of some rice plants has increased by 700%.

Tea clipper

In the 1700s and 1800s ships – tea clippers – brought tea to Britain from India. Foreign money was needed to develop tea plantations. It takes four years before a tea bush will produce leaves for tea.

Rice terraces
Cutting terraces in hillsides allows farmers to grow crops on land that would otherwise be inaccessible. Terraces are edged with walls, normally built of stone, to hold back water to create the flooded conditions rice needs to grow.

Rice harvesting
Farming for rice is hard work — it is planted by hand, harvested by hand and many people are needed to cultivate it. But now machines have been developed to do some of the work.

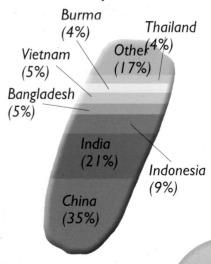

World's rice producers

Burma (4%)
Thailand (4%)
Vietnam (5%)
Other (17%)
Bangladesh (5%)
India (21%)
Indonesia (9%)
China (35%)

Colourful religions

India, the world's second most populous nation, has given the world two major religions – Buddhism and Hinduism. Today, Buddhists are found mainly in Thailand, Sri Lanka, Burma, Cambodia, China and Japan rather than India where it began. But in India the majority now follows Hinduism, which is probably the oldest major religion in the world. The Asian countries where Buddhism is a major religion are increasingly Westernised – particularly Japan and Thailand. Both Hindus and Buddhists have ornate temples. The region also has many Muslims – Indonesia has the biggest Muslim population.

Chinese New Year
Although China is in Northern Asia, many Chinese live in Southeast Asia. These communities celebrate Chinese New Year, with festivals which include the 'dragon dance'.

Gods and goddesses

Hindus believe in a great god called Vishnu, a destroyer god (Shiva) and a goddess (Devi). These gods take many different forms and there are hundreds of minor gods. Temples are dedicated to particular gods.

Holy lives

Many Buddhists follow a monk's life, even if only for a time. It is, thus, perfectly normal for men to become monks for a short while. They wear yellow robes and carry food bowls with which they seek donations from the public.

Holy Cow

To Hindus, cows are held to be sacred and allowed to wander undisturbed, even in towns. India has more cattle than any other country. Although cows are milked, Hindus never kill cows to eat. One Indian in 10 is vegetarian, and never eats any meat.

The rainy season

The countries in southern Asia are near enough to the tropics to be hot. Southeast Asia, near the Equator, has a climate like the tropical rainforest of Africa – hot and wet all year round. But India and Bangladesh, which are farther north, have more seasonal variation. In summer, when the Sun is overhead, central Asia gets very hot – it is too far inland for the sea to cool it down. Hot air rises over central Asia and, to take its place, cooler air is drawn in from over the Indian Ocean. This air has travelled a long way over the sea and so is very moist. When it reaches hills in India, Pakistan and Bangladesh it is pushed up, and cools down to give huge quantities of rain. This wet season is called the monsoon.

Weather in Bombay, India

Average temperature:
25°C – December
29°C – June

Average rainfall:
508 mm – December
0 mm – June

Palm-fringed beaches
Large stretches of the coast of southern Asia are lined with dense vegetation that thrives in the tropical climate.

Wildlife
High temperatures and heavy rainfall encourage forests to grow. In the dry season, tropical grasses flourish. These habitats suit the Indian elephant.

Climate zones
- Mountains
- Temperate
- Tropical rainforest
- Desert

Weather patterns
Monsoon winds blow over India from the south-west between April and October. Before this, the weather is very hot and dry. People long for the rains to come, to cool the air and help the rice crop to grow.

Wettest in the world
When the very wet air carried by monsoon winds reaches India and Bangladesh, it is forced to rise over hills (left). As it rises, the air cools, and deposits the moisture as rain. The wettest place in the world is Cherrapungi in north-east India, where once 26,461 mm of rain fell in one year.

Evaporation due to Sun

Air forced to rise

Monsoon reaches land

CLIMATE

Old and new

Oceania is dominated by Australia and New Zealand, two modern countries where life is much as it is in Britain or USA. The tiny island nations of the Pacific are also Westernised. But although the majority of people in Oceania are Christian, there are still ancient religions known as 'primal religions'. Primal means 'first' , because these religions were there long before the major world religions arrived. People who follow primal religions usually believe in a supreme god, but also many other lesser gods and spirits, and honour their ancestors.

Maoris

In New Zealand, three people in every 20 are Maoris, the original inhabitants. Most Maoris are now town-dwellers and the traditional houses (right) are very few.

Uluru

Uluru (once called Ayers Rock), is known as the 'red heart' of Australia. This massive rock – nearly 350 m high and over 3.5 km long – is one of the most sacred sites of Australia's aborigines. It changes colour according to the direction of the Sun.

Aboriginal artefacts

The Aborigines of Australia once had no fixed homes and wandered Australia hunting and gathering roots and fruit. The Aborigines drew colourful rock paintings and carved boomerangs and other objects.

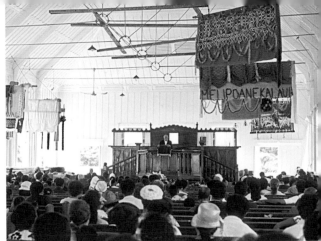

Pacific worship

The Pacific islands have been largely Christian for 100 years. But because each island or group of islands often received missionaries from just one Church, today many island groups belong mainly to one religion – Tonga, for example, is Methodist.

Different types of land

The Pacific Ocean covers just over one third of the world. Stretched across this ocean is the world's smallest continent, Oceania, made up of thousands of islands. Some are the tops of mountains or volcanoes, others have been built by coral. But in the vast Pacific, islands occupy less than 1% of the total area. Alongside these small islands are four larger ones – Australia, the world's largest island, New Guinea and the North and South Islands of New Zealand. Between them, these four islands have a remarkable variety of scenery including high, jagged mountains, dense tropical jungles, barren icy hills, wide sandy deserts and fertile sub-tropical lowlands.

Opening in Earth's crust

Coral Atoll Islands

Many Oceanian islands are made of coral. These islands, in the form of long reefs and round atolls, develop when coral grows up in shallow tropical seas. The Great Barrier Reef, at 2027 km long, is the largest living structure on Earth. The largest coral atoll, Kwajalein in the Marshall Islands, encloses a huge lagoon within its outer ring of 'land'.

Volcano formation

Volcanoes are mountains built up above an opening in the Earth's crust. Through this opening, molten rock (magma) wells up and is often thrown out with great force. Most volcanoes occur along the edges of the world's plates and a ring of volcanoes lines the Pacific Ocean. Volcanoes can erupt under the sea (left) and sometimes surface in Oceania as new islands.

Molten rock wells up

Volcano erupts

New Zealand

Where molten rock is close to the ground it can heat up underground water. This produces hot springs, which are common in volcanic regions such as the Rotorua region of the North Island of New Zealand. Some hot springs called geysers eject hot water and steam in sudden spectacular eruptions. There are also boiling mud pools. These volcanic features attract tourists and the natural hot water is used for heating houses.

'Discovery' of Oceania

Our history books usually tell us about the discovery of the islands of Oceania by Spanish, Dutch and British navigators, such as Magellan and Cook. But these islands had already been discovered, and settled, by Polynesians, Melanesians and Micronesians who originally came from Asia more than 2000 years ago. When Europeans reached Oceania 500 years ago, they found these peoples established as farmers and fishermen. The Micronesian Maoris reached New Zealand 1000 years before Europeans.

Key to map routes

▬▬▬	1492 Christopher Columbus
▬▬▬	1497–98 Vasco Da Gama
▬▬▬	1519–21 Magellan
▬ ▬ ▬	Completed by Del Cano 1522
▬▬▬	1768–71 James Cook

Working abroad

The small Pacific nations have rapidly increasing populations and there is not enough work for everyone. So, large numbers of people are leaving the Oceanian islands to work in New Zealand, the USA and Australia. Some islands have more people living abroad than they do at home. The Cook Islands (above) have a population of 18,000 but there are another 21,000 Cook Islanders working in New Zealand.

Tiny new countries

Oceania is a region of young countries. Over the last 100 years, the island nations have been colonies of the US, Britain, France, Japan and Germany – and later, Australia and New Zealand too. Since the 1960s, groups of islands such as Fiji have become independent. These small countries have few resources. Most rely upon economic help from the countries that used to rule them, but the islands now aim for greater independence by working closely with each other.

Island kingdom

Tonga is an independent, very traditional, island nation. Every male Tongan is entitled to three hectares of land when he becomes 16 but – owing to a rapidly expanding population – this right is under threat. Here, Tongan women are making bark cloth – an ancient, traditional craft of the island.

Youthful city

Australia is the 'oldest' country in Oceania, having been founded in 1901. Sydney, Australia's biggest city, is only 200 years old. It is home to people from all over the world – immigrants from many parts of Europe, Oceania and Asia.

CHANGING WORLD

Threat to islands

The rise in industry, particularly in North America, northern Europe, China and Japan, has brought wealth but it has also created problems. Smoke from industrial chimneys releases harmful chemicals into the air. Car exhaust fumes add to the pollution. But it is the 'greenhouse effect' and global warming that are the biggest danger. Ice in the polar regions will melt and raise sea levels. By 2050, the sea will have risen by about 50 cm and the islands of Oceania will begin to suffer. A rise of one metre would drown nearly all of the nation of Tuvalu and most of its neighbour Kiribati.

Reef damage
Coral reefs may look robust. But coral (right) is fragile — formed from the 'skeletons' of tiny creatures — and easily damaged by fishing. Polluted water and an increase in sea temperature, owing to global warming, have killed billions of the tiny creatures that make coral. As a result, more than one third of the world's coral reefs is now dead.

Sun's rays

carbon dioxide in atmosphere

some heat is reflected back into space

heat trapped inside the atmosphere

heat penetrates atmosphere to reach Earth's surface

Islands lying low

Oceania consists of thousands of small low-lying islands made from coral. Many of these islands may disappear under the waves of the Pacific Ocean as sea level rises because the planet is getting warmer. The islanders will have to find new homes, probably in the USA, New Zealand and Australia where many people have already moved from the more overcrowded islands.

The greenhouse effect

Carbon dioxide is released into the atmosphere by burning coal and oil (fossil fuels). This gas threatens the environment by making the Earth's atmosphere warmer. This is known as the greenhouse effect (above) because carbon dioxide in the atmosphere acts like glass in a greenhouse. Just as glass traps heat inside, so carbon dioxide traps heat in the atmosphere.

Polluted beaches

The small islands of Oceania have a problem disposing of waste and sewage and have sometimes resorted to dumping it at sea. The result has been unpleasant pollution of beaches and sea water and also the death of some of the fish and other marine life.

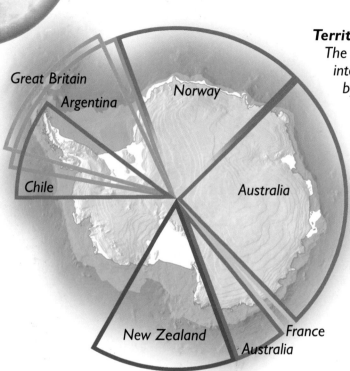

Great Britain
Argentina
Norway
Chile
Australia
New Zealand
France
Australia

Territorial claims
The map (left) shows the current international claims on Antarctica made by seven countries.

Scientific research
Antarctica has important scientific bases. The Scott-Amundsen Base (below) near the South Pole is one of the largest. Weather stations tell us much about the world's climate, geologists look for minerals and astronomers take advantage of Antarctica's clear skies.

Disputed boundaries
Antarctica is home to bases established by 19 different countries. Various chunks of Antarctica are claimed by seven different countries – Britain, Australia, New Zealand, Norway, France, Chile and Argentina – and in places these claims overlap. Ownership of the land may one day become important because of possible mineral deposits.

Final frontier

Before the 20th century the polar regions – the areas around the North Pole and the frozen continent of Antarctica – were largely uninhabited and even unexplored. The polar regions are the world's 'last frontier'. The climate is harsh – in many areas the snow and ice never melt. But there have been good reasons for people to brave the cold – to further research and search for new mineral sources.

Robert Scott

The British naval officer Robert Scott (right) commanded two Antarctic expeditions, but died on his return journey from the Pole in 1912. He had been beaten to the Pole by the Norwegian explorer Roald Amundsen. French and Russian explorers also played an important part in mapping Antarctica.

Mines

The polar wastes of Antarctica and the Arctic islands were some of the last areas on Earth to remain untouched by humans. But even here – and in the far north of Russia, North America and in Greenland – human activity is damaging nature. Scientists search for valuable minerals in these frozen places, as deposits begin to be used up elsewhere. The United States is now having difficulty supplying enough oil and natural gas for its needs. Large-scale development is taking place in northern Alaska to extract these fuels, even though the area is protected.

Food for whales

Whales are not confined to Arctic and Antarctic waters, but many species spend time there, feeding on plankton and other tiny creatures that thrive in cold seas. As the Earth heats up due to global warming, this rich food source may become threatened, in turn affecting the whales.

Blue whale

Midnight sun

Near the poles, the Sun is visible at midnight in summer. Tourists are attracted to view the 'midnight Sun'. Conservationists fear that the small, but growing, number of tourists to polar regions may damage an almost untouched environment.

Protecting our environment

High up in the Earth's atmosphere, the ozone layer acts like a filter, protecting us from harmful radiation from the Sun. Gases that were once used in aerosol sprays and refrigerators (CFCs) and fire extinguishers (halons) were very damaging to this ozone.
A hole in the ozone layer above Antarctica was first noticed in 1985, and continued to grow in size. Scientists realized what was causing this to happen and as a result, governments worldwide decided to ban the use of CFCs and halons.

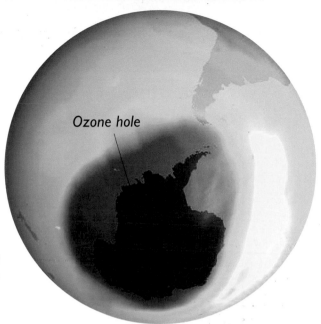

Ozone hole

Icebergs

In the last 25 years the ice sheets at the North and South Poles have been melting, due to global warming. Larger chunks of ice have been breaking away from the icecaps to form icebergs.

Rocky coasts

There is evidence in polar regions to show that human activity is changing the Earth's climate. The planet is getting warmer, causing the ice in Antarctica, Greenland and around the North Pole to melt. Bare rock is already showing along some of the coasts of Antarctica, where before there was thick ice.

ENVIRONMENT

POLAR REGIONS

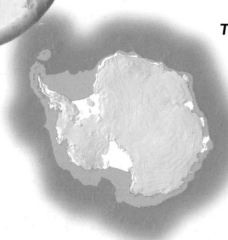

The coldest pole

Antarctica is generally colder than the Arctic because it is more mountainous. The coldest temperature ever recorded was at the Russian Antarctic scientific base Vostok, in 1983, when the temperature fell to nearly -83°C.

Summer in the Arctic

In northern Russia and Canada is a snowy landscape called tundra. Ice in the soil melts during summer, making the land into a boggy marsh.

Changing lifestyle

The Inuits of northern Canada and Greenland once lived in igloos – small round houses made of ice blocks. Today, igloos are only made as temporary shelters. Many Inuits, particularly in Greenland, live in flats in towns.

Tropic of Cancer

Tropic of Capricorn

Cold extremes

The polar regions are too far from the Equator for the Sun ever to be overhead, or for there to be much seasonal difference in temperature.

Cold air descending

In polar regions, cold air from higher up in the atmosphere drops down to the Earth's surface. At surface level, this cold air flows away from the poles. There is no warm air blowing in from the south to ease the severity of the cold wind. The sea around Antarctica and the Arctic freezes over during winter, when it is coldest. In the past in Antarctica, the frozen ice appeared to almost double the size of the continent. But as the planet warms up due to global warming the amount of frozen sea around Antarctica is getting smaller.

Dry ice

The polar regions are called ice deserts. The air there is very dry. No moist air can be drawn in from the surrounding oceans to fill the space usually left by warm air rising. The little rain that does fall is frozen – snow.

Permanent camps

At any one time, there are scientific expeditions from more than 25 countries happening in the Arctic and Antarctica. Scientists may set up temporary camps, such as the one above, but permanent underground bases provide better protection against the cold.

Weather in Longyearbyen

 Average temperature:
-15°C – December
2°C – June

Average rainfall/snow:
38 mm, snow –
December
10 mm – June

Demand for minerals

Wherever there are minerals worth extracting, mining will occur. One day it might be worthwhile to extract natural wealth from under the icecaps of the North Pole and Antarctica – but not yet. It is not worthwhile mining in polar regions because it costs too much to recover minerals in such harsh conditions. But when we run out of minerals elsewhere we will have to resort to mining polar regions.

Satellite survey

Hidden reserves of minerals can be found by surveying magnetically. A large deposit of iron is like a magnet. Surveying can be done from the air by plane or satellite.

Hidden resources

Occasionally ores – bodies of minerals – can be seen on the surface. But in the polar regions ores are hidden not only by layers of rock but under ice and snow.

Difficult conditions

If mining is ever to take place in Antarctica, a whole new type of mining industry will have to be invented. Working at such low temperatures, the ground will be frozen and difficult to dig. And exporting minerals by sea would be a problem when the sea is frozen around Antarctica for much of the year. Cargo ships would have to be designed as icebreakers, like the one shown below, with special hulls that can smash through the ice sheet.

Potential polar resources

Lead and zinc used to be mined in Greenland, but it is now too expensive to dig out what is left. Coal has been found under the frozen land of Svalbard, a group of Norwegian islands in the Arctic Circle. There is natural gas under Ellesmere Island and the Queen Elizabeth Islands far to the north of Canada. And the same islands have zinc and lead deposits. But they are not recovered — yet.

Minerals in Antarctica

The large deposits of coal found in the Transantarctic Mountains would be too expensive to mine.

Evidence of iron ore has been found in the Transantarctic Mountains.

Gold has been found in small amounts in Queen Maud Land.

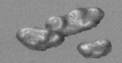

Copper has been traced in the Antarctic peninsula.

Natural Gas has been found in the Ross Sea.

NATURAL RICHES

GLOSSARY

Agriculture The process of cultivating the land. eg growing crops.

Atmosphere The layer of air, 700 km deep, that surrounds the Earth.

Climate The term given to types of weather over a period of time.

Colony An area of land ruled by another country.

Drought A long period of dry weather without rain.

Equator An imaginary line around the Earth, equal in distance between the North and South Poles.

Erosion The process of wearing away the Earth's surface – mainly caused by water, wind and ice.

Export The sale of goods to another country.

Fault A break or line of weakness in the Earth's crust.

Global warming The increase in the Earth's temperature caused by too much carbon dioxide in the atmosphere.

Habitat The particular area or natural place where a group of plants or animals live.

Irrigation The watering of the land by artificial methods, usually to help the growth of food crops.

Plantation An area of land used to grow plants, such as cotton and tea, to be harvested and sold.

Plate The Earth's crust is divided into about 15 huge pieces called plates.

Pollution Damage to the environment caused by human activity.

Refugee A person who flees to another country for shelter or protection.

Reservoir A man-made lake or tank used to store water.

Satellite A small body that orbits round a larger one. Earth has one satellite – the Moon. There are also hundreds of artificial satellites orbiting the Earth.

Shanty town An area where housing is makeshift.

Westernized To become like the people of Europe or America in customs, ideas or practices.

INDEX